Just Down the Road

poems by

Dee Stribling

Finishing Line Press
Georgetown, Kentucky

Just Down the Road

Copyright © 2017 by Dee Stribling
ISBN 978-1-63534-263-5 First Edition
All rights reserved under International and Pan-American Copyright Conventions.
No part of this book may be reproduced in any manner whatsoever without written permission from the publisher, except in the case of brief quotations embodied in critical articles and reviews.

ACKNOWLEDGMENTS

Dawn Shamp and Joseph Bathanti for your incredible support and assistance.

My Table Rock poet friends for your patience and unending belief in me. Each of you is a gift in my life—Sue Dunlap, Laurie Wilcox-Meyer, and Kim Blum-Hyclak.

Marty Harris for again sharing a wonderful cover photograph.

And to those dear to me who understand the arts and writing life—Judy, Dea, Nancy, Kim, Connie, Hannah, and family.

Publisher: Leah Maines

Editor: Christen Kincaid

Cover Art: Marty Harris

Author Photo: Judy Long

Cover Design: Elizabeth Maines McCleavy

Printed in the USA on acid-free paper.
Order online: www.finishinglinepress.com
also available on amazon.com

Author inquiries and mail orders:
Finishing Line Press
P. O. Box 1626
Georgetown, Kentucky 40324
U. S. A.

Table of Contents

Roads 1

Poppy's Handprints 2

Staying Over 3

Bobcat 4

Friends 5

Caleb's Eyes 6

Sweet Water 7

Plymouth 8

Healing 9

John Short 10

Hot Water Heater 11

Holler 12

Grandpa on the Porch 13

Bread 14

Papa's Memory 15

Day Spent 16

Solace 17

Prayer for Ida-Mae 18

The Color of Payne's Gray 19

Going Home 20

This book is dedicated to my foothills and mountain family and friends. Your unfailing warmth, humor, strength, and love has carried me through hard times and helped me celebrate the good. Your presence in my life is a blessing beyond words. Thank you.

ROADS

Ask of my dream and I'll tell you a lie
    until I go there and meet the people
    and watch their horizon appear over
    farms, rivers, mountains, snow.

Until I hear the wind screaming through
    Ida-Mae's holler and howling across Short's
    field as it picks up packs of sounds from
    coyotes, bobcats, owls.

Until the yellow sun blazes into cinders of night
    with white moonlit clouds showing the
    way across fields full of pricked ears
    waiting for the tiniest rustle of grasses.

Yes, ask me of my dream until I can tell you
    with all my being that my heart found
    temporary lodging there and spirit, earth,
    and sky were comfortable and welcoming.

POPPY'S HANDPRINTS

Little girl laughter fills the air as she
runs through fields of yellow flowers
and tall meadow grasses under blue
sky full of soft summer white clouds.

Old home awaits—planks and porch
cracked and falling. Tin roof failing.
She runs to the back, following morning
glory trail to an old window.

She looks inside to see a small
swirl of dust in the air from an
old rocker—moving as if someone
has just arisen and walked away.

She wants to be inside, but the old
window won't give way to little hands.
On tiptoes looking in is the only way to
join the old house and its memories.

She watches until wind begins to stir in
the big oak. Spell broken, she turns and
quickly runs away. Small handprints on a
window the only testament to her stay.

STAYING OVER

Sometimes Ida-Mae spent nights at her grandparents' house.
When small, she slept downstairs in her grandma's room.
Trees outside the windows loomed tall and dark,
moonlight sent limb and leaf shadows onto the wall.

When older, Ida-Mae stayed upstairs in her grandpa's room.
Slanted alcove above the porch still held his scent and clothes.
She loved his old shirts, all blue plaids and stripes.
His pipe lay beside the bed waiting for him.

Muffled voices—laughter and conversations
floated upstairs like music. When voices grew quiet, footsteps
would begin, one boot in front of the other. Creaking up the stairs,
turning at the landing, stopping outside her bedroom door.

Ida-Mae waited for the soft touch on her shoulder as unseen
hands tucked the patchwork quilt up around her neck.
Wrapped in her grandpa's oldest blue shirt, she slept,
dreams carrying her on night's journey far, far away.

BOBCAT

I first heard screams the night grandpa's barn burned down.
A fiery red sky reflected like a pool of blood in the lake.
Did bobcat know what was about to happen? Was there a scent?
Some first smell of smoke? Or was it that the panic of animals
swept like a wave of fear across field and woods?

All the rest of summer I woke up just before it started.
Dark and heavy silence pressed close to my face,
seconds counted in minutes until the screaming began.
The sound would go on and on, first from the row of cedar trees,
then on toward the lake. It tore apart the night, reaching
deep inside, filling me so full of fear I could barely breathe.

The neighbor's chickens and guinea were all gone in one night.
There was no going out after dark that summer.
Not sure who or what was lurking above my head or following
just out of sight. The cedars turned a dark, waxy green
that melted into black nights, hiding something to be feared.

Over the winter the screaming stopped as suddenly as it started.
No tracks in the snow, no mists of warm breath suspended in air.
No unseen yellow eyes watching me or leaving tufts of spotted fur
on the fencepost. Nothing. Gone except for the torn parts left
behind from the kill.

FRIENDS

Poppy, Ida-Mae, and me sitting pretty like clothespins on a line.
Feet reaching for old rug on the floor, like we were trying to hold
up a sheet blowing in the wind.

Three of us growing up
sharing secrets all the way.
Who put gum under the table?
Rode bareback flying across the field?
Which of us got married and then
carried away in Charlie's '57 Chevy?

Blossoms blown into the air from one dandelion stem.
Raising families, living life, till two found our way home again.
Wearing white gloves and little hats,
Dresses below our knees, walking through family names
faded now in winter's graves.
Who will be the next of us to go? And who will linger on?
What stories will be told when we meet again beyond?

Poppy, Ida-Mae, and me sitting pretty like clothespins on a line.

CALEB'S EYES

She'd remember him if she ever saw him again.
Blue eyes framed in white with dark center.
Looking at him was looking into black night sky.

He took her breath away. Completely. Words
were gone, too. He asked if she'd been to Roan
Mountain because that's where he lived, halfway up.

She said she hadn't, but she'd been to Mitchell
and hiked Table Rock and Hawksbill. He looked
at her and said, "Roan's the prettiest."

Then, just as she was gonna answer, he spun
round on his heel and just started walking off.
Too many words. She'd visit Roan Mountain soon.

Maybe there are wolves there, maybe they
have blue eyes framed in white with dark center.
Maybe she'll just listen to them and not talk.

SWEET WATER

He looks like he just has one hand.

The other, hidden underneath, curls
around the porch rail like the runner
from a warm sweet potato body.

Barefoot and dirt-stained legs happy
with summer sweat, dangle.

She's home noon from work in the field.
Picking peas in her pink gingham dress.

Charlie thinks she's pretty.

He's the one sitting there watching
with a little smile, knowing he's way
too young yet, but that he'll catch
up to her.

She sees Charlie smile.
Sipping cool spring water, she knows
one day he'll make some woman
a good husband.

Sweet water, soothing day's sun.

She wipes her mouth with the back
of her hand, tosses her hair
and sends a blue-eyed smile
his way   just one.

PLYMOUTH

Charlie takes me with him to North Wilkesboro.

At sixteen years old no one suspects me.
Innocence in the front seat protecting all
that liquor stored in the trunk tank.

He was used to thundering past the grandstands
and people standing way too close to the track
just hoping for the speed to rub off on them.

Standing now by the old Plymouth I know
I'm just one step away from Highway 421
and flying past corn fields, cows, and tobacco.

We come around corners on two wheels
with those port-o-walls glowing white against
the headlights on this dark country road.

He's bringing a load of whiskey back to sell
and I get to prime bottles instead of tobacco.
Charlie floors it while I hang on to a grin and the door.

HEALING

Poppy's mama could talk the fire out of a burn.
I've seen her do it. She comforted little girl screams
from a burning cinder and there weren't no mark left
on that little girl's arm.

I can make warts go away from anywhere.
Will take a couple of days after I do whatever I do,
but I promise that even the biggest batch of warts
will just disappear for good.

Ida-Mae's mama was a midwife. She lived across the
Toe River and was who got called for birthing. Even
the rich town women called on her. She comforted
them and their new little ones.

Ida-Mae lives in a big old white house. She was
a nurse at a teaching hospital in Asheville. They
studied her once because her patients got better
quicker than anyone else's.

And Poppy is who you call if you have haints
and shadows in your house. She knows how
to talk to them so they quiet down and don't
drive the living crazy.

Caleb knows all about plants. He and his
grandma both understood what to pick and when
and how to dry it or make a poultice or a tea
but whatever you took in, it healed you.

We grew up with healing. That's just the way it was.

JOHN SHORT

John Short comes back to me in dreams.

His big, rough hands stoked coal fires
for moonshine days and drunken nights.

He used to say, "Sweet pea, them crows
sure are talking this morning."

Sleek black feather-backs catching the sun.
Sharing words spoken in croaks and whistles;
They perch, four of them, talking away.
They might as well have spectacles and cigars.
Something moves at a distance—perhaps a hawk?
Four piercing stares as wind sends sweet gum
balls to the ground. They turn on their branches
and watch the sky, stopping conversation for just
this moment. Then, with great fluffing of feathers,
they resume their visit and crow stories.

Small pleasures for hard times.

John and I would watch together.
His suspenders frayed, collarless shirt
stained with rivulets of tobacco juice.

Broken down boots still standing.

HOT WATER HEATER

Papa and me threw an old
hot water heater down the bank.

Used to be the country way.
Dumped over the edge to lie
fallow until the first weed tendril
found a foothold and began
creeping up the side.

Kudzu and mushrooms, damp
fallen leaves, nursed by rain
and mist, a lively team of players
always arrives to feed on rust,
paint, and tangled insides.

Don't push or roll over.
Copperheads strike quick
in their own rust-colored work
suits from this perfect place
to curl and rest and wait.

Laugh when the city folks
come country to buy up
old property and look
puzzled, wondering why a
hot water tank lives in the woods.

Because we threw it there.
Wasn't any other thing to do
with it or any of the other trash
that wouldn't burn down like
the leaf pile to wet smokiness.

Old tank and fixtures
will outlive us all. She'll be
there as a white sail in the
woods, a Christopher Columbus
new world for all things small.

HOLLER

Papa would holler through day
on into night,
white lightning's song
was his delight.
We kids first ran away
until we learned with each note
his reach and run would end up
facedown on pine porch planks.

GRANDPA ON THE PORCH

You stand there, thumbs under bib overall snaps,
waiting to see which grandkid gets to you first.
Running up the dirt road, ten bare feet kick up dust.

Two kids to the well dipper, two onto cane-bottom
porch chairs, one hugging you just above your knees.
Then, all scatter—like leaves blowing away in the wind.

Old oak tree, bent over with the weight of winter ice,
summer storms, and memories, sighs a troubled breeze.
She knows you're fading, but we don't own up to it.

She sees you go from brown to pale, blue bib overalls
worn too thin to stand even the smallest tear.
Now, you've completely gone away, cloth to bone to dust.

But your place on the porch is always open.
Not one of us ever moves a chair or rocker over it.
Even visitors walk around where you used to be.

BREAD

I remember bread, baked and warm from the oven.
Sometimes in a flat cake pan, cinnamon sugar drizzled over it.
Baking while the sugar melted running sweetness all through the dough.

I remember scrambled eggs and my papa
in faded blue shirts and overalls.
Every workday at breakfast—eggs, bacon, bread, and coffee.
I rode with him to school until the day I didn't.
He dropped dead at the factory.

Mama dealt with this for a while—continued to bake bread
and make breakfast and take me to school and pick me up.
Until she couldn't.

We found a new home in town.
By morning we left our house in the country.
By evening all that had come to live within my heart was gone.

PAPA'S MEMORY

Yesterday, sitting at breakfast,
I thought of my papa.
Somewhere between bacon and grits,
sadness wrapped itself around me,
comfortable and familiar,
like an old shirt worn long ago.
I don't know where papa is buried.
I don't know where his ashes are.
The wooden box with the urn
that sat between the feet
of a thirteen-year-old is gone.
Memory of an endless rocking
train through the mountains
and image of my mama crying
during the long gray car ride
to a small cemetery is not.
I watched her watch some man
I didn't know bury the box
that held the ashes of the man I knew.
The cemetery was overgrown then.
It would be impossible to find now.

DAY SPENT

Ida-Mae and Caleb spoke in quiet
April mornings sprinkled with blue
cornflowers waving in soft breezes
across fields of spring wheat.

They worked together as summer
sunlit days stretched to meet
mourning dove calls at dusk;
corn growing toward deep blue sky.

Ida-Mae can still feel his hand
in autumn as she walks field stubble
left for rabbits and deer, looking back
while evening light begins to settle.

This day, as she senses winter's
coming, he has journeyed to
a bright light she has yet to know, but
will not fear on her walk back home.

SOLACE

Poppy wants the safety of home.
Looking down at her supper, with no
one around her, there's no need
for dinner conversation or laughter.
Family gone, their lives now apart
from hers in the greater passing world.

She remembers looking across the table
while her children lifted fork to mouth
with chicken-fried steak, fresh lima beans,
and Silver Queen corn dripping butter.
All taking pleasure in the gift of food
grace placed before them.

But now, she is tired. The rush of this
world has become too much. She wants to
leave all that's not part of her sweet water
behind. Leave years of pain scattered along
life's roadside like so many clothes freed
from a broken suitcase.

History with family gone leaves only her
to keep memories. Finding solace in simple
things, she sits, her gaze fixed upon an empty
plate glazed with the remnants of life's feast.
She is ready for all to be cleared from the table,
washed clean and put away.

PRAYER FOR IDA-MAE

Call cold across the mountain,
snowy cedar lace-laden limbs
crossed over sheltering the small.

She looks out across the valley,
sees the fog swirling up,
consuming all living things.

Lord, lift her up to the clouds,
send her spirit into the sky
on your winds and light.

Let the stars come down
like snowflakes to swirl about
her face and light her path.

Trust that she won't fall,
the honeysuckle path is gone,
vines now brittle in winter.

Trust that white blossoms
return in the spring, even
without her here to see them.

THE COLOR OF PAYNE'S GRAY

I remember the gray.
The soft plait of mama's hair.
Divide into thirds, top over middle.
Mornings framed in dust motes, kitchen clatter,
coffee, chipped beef on toast.

Padding softly, carrying a plate to sit and look.
Watch steers through early mist take the old path
through broom sage.
Bluets float in an old salt pinch pot,
tiny vase lost on oilcloth flowers.
Sip of coffee, bite of toast and gravy.
Sunbeams creep over the windowsill.

I sit now in the gray.
Evening light filters through the old window.
A crow comes to peck, curious about the reflection he saw
from his broken limb. I look up, hands folded on my lap.
Grandmother clock ticks away the minutes it takes
for me to fall away.

Memories swirl and lift.
Babies born, children who lived and married. Friends.
Love beneath apple trees through sweet summer blossoms
and fall gatherings. Flowers yellow and pink lift as sweet
smells of lilac and honeysuckle fill night air.
All is empty now, gone away.

GOING HOME

Bells toll across the valley
    their sound muted by steep slopes
    and sadness running down clear-cuts
    until both settle like fog across cabin and town.

She sits up with family
    silver coins over her eyes no longer seeing
    but still there watching as sister, brother, mother, father
    all come round to guard, stay, and offer respects.

Waiting for three days
    all in black so the shades can't tell the living
    but they are all there with her anyway, the ones
    who've gone before but only she can see them now.

Her head will be west
    and her feet will be east, she'll hear the praise songs,
    she'll watch as the earth she loved so much falls
    gently from shovel to grave but she won't be there.

Tears will beat down like rain
    while friends and family gather round home's table
    filled now with pots of beans and meat, pies and cakes
    washed down and finished with shuffling good-byes.

She'll hear her horse's hooves
    as he comes across the field, waits for her at the gate
    until he feels her slip onto his back then, his mane flying
    in the mist, he'll take her over the pasture and back home.

Dee Stribling is a writer of prose and poetry. A Sundress Academy for the Arts poetry winner her work has appeared in *200 New Mexico Poems* and other collections. Additional poetry chapbooks include *Appalachian Picture Book* (Finishing Line Press) and *Down East Picture Book* (Horse & Buggy Press). Work in-progress includes a childhood memoir and more poetry. Her documentary about "The Why Nots" softball team (with Minnow Media) is slated for release soon. You can visit her online at www.facebook.com/PoetDStribling and www.deestribling.com.

www.ingramcontent.com/pod-product-compliance
Lightning Source LLC
LaVergne TN
LVHW041523070426
835507LV00012B/1792